LIFELINES

Duncan Forbes

LIFELINES

Duncan Forbes

21 February 2017

ENITHARMON PRESS

First published in 2009
by Enitharmon Press
26B Caversham Road
London NW5 2DU

www.enitharmon.co.uk

Distributed in the UK by
Central Books
99 Wallis Road
London E9 5LN

Distributed in the USA and Canada
by Dufour Editions Inc.
PO Box 7, Chester Springs
PA 19425, USA

ISBN: 978-1-904634-65-2

Enitharmon Press gratefully acknowledges the financial support of
Arts Council England, London.

British Library Cataloguing-in-Publication Data.
A catalogue record for this book is available
from the British Library.

Designed in Albertina by Libanus Press
and printed in England by
Antony Rowe Ltd

The poems in this selection are drawn from the following books:

Poetry Introduction 5	Faber	1982
August Autumn	Secker and Warburg	1984
Public & Confidential	Enitharmon Press	1989
Taking Liberties	Enitharmon Press	1993
Voice Mail	Enitharmon Press	2002
Vision Mixer	Enitharmon Press	2006

CONTENTS

from *Vision Mixer* (2006)

AT THE REGAL

Is there nothing better to do
On a Monday afternoon
Than watch a film about caribou
Waiting for the western to come on?
I munch sweets in the stalls and think
This is the worst film I have ever seen
As the caribou migrate across
Acres of tundra on the screen,
Cold, tired and cadaverous
And as near as makes no odds extinct.

In preference to junk like that
Give me the cowboy any day –
Living where he hangs his goddam hat
And playing poker for his pay –
Yup, he could make me a brand new man
If he just complied with three small ifs:
1) if he had acne on his chin,
2) he were a part-time pacifist
And 3) he once had to ask the heroine
'Say, honey, sorry, where's the can?'

That's the sort of thing I want,
Loads of authenticity:
Viz. The couple courting hard in front
Whose stifled brute activity
Excites me more than every horde
Of Hollywood Apache braves
Repelled by the US Cavalry.
Those lovers can at least paraphrase
Both my lust and jealousy,
And they aren't either hired or bored.

A NAVAL WIFE

A naval wife, driving her husband's car,
Heads for an art materials shop, to get
A blown-up photo of his carrier framed.
It shows, he wrote, the flight-deck plus a jet.
Hoped to fit more water in but I mis-aimed.

She parks by a seagull-pestered reservoir,
A type-cast backcloth for a town, half port
Half shopping-centre cum resort. The gulls
Yelling above her prompt her to recall
Dockyards at dawn, gloom, then the carrier hull's
Long shadow sliding down the jetty: all
Things which the snapshot had by proxy caught.

PREP SCHOOL GROUNDS

Each of the trees in Kennedy's gender rhymes
Plus many non-Indo-European species
Grew Latin nameplateless in the school grounds.
So the first trees we learnt there were as climbs,
Not masculine, feminine or neuter nouns.
Balsa alone came extra to the fees
From an Aylesbury shop in precut pieces,
But otherwise all other then-known trees
Had either bark or branches we could grip –
All but the sumachs which were out of bounds.
    Yews blackened sweat and inked in palmistries,
The cedars leaked a sap like balsa glue.
Redwoods we sprinted at with skewers of box,
Each trying to stab the trunk highest with his.
We used scots pine branches to sweep an airstrip
From which, between an ash and conker tree,
Holding toy planes to fircone bombs we flew.
But the only play in the woods there that connected
Genders and trees were games of Off-ground He
Where the headmaster's daughter, Rosalind,
Was too slow to be worthwhile making It.
    Her father taught us later in Top Form
With our long trouser turn-ups full of twigs
That though there were exceptions to the norm
French trees were male and Latin feminine,
And here for once he thought the Romans right.
The tallest trees, climbed only by the wind,
Were what I fell for: elms at their full height
Were substantives that made me adjectival,
Without attracting me in a sexual way.
For though those elm trees, pines and poplars lent

The school its *Graf Spee* on the skyline shapes
For miles around, they supervised survival,
Since they'd endured from that long holiday
Before each bedroom had become a dorm,
Before the wallbars and the fire escapes.

THE FIFTH COLUMN

The Fifth Column
between my legs
the mauve toad
with hairy eggs
garlic sausage
with an appetite,
my magic wand
of dynamite,
has this minute
commissioned me
to write his auto-
biography.

DEPOSITION

Christ's body smelt of Goddard's Silver Dip
When as head prefect not as sacristan
I carried at school Eucharists the cross
Up to the gilt one on the reredos
Where as a new boy near the servers' stalls
I had admired, compelled to be at worship,
Those mutually exclusive optionals
Of Art and Carpentry in unison.

But outside chapel crucifixions hurt.
They tied you by the wrists to clothing hooks
Which kept your head still so you could be gagged
With a taste of hand, until you'd been debagged.
Compared to this, I saw Christ crucified
In terms that sermon cricket could convert
To signalling a universal Wide,
Which I still bowl and on which he still looks.

For, seeing a woman on a London bus
Each of whose earlobes was a crucifer,
Since flat gold crosses dangled from her ears
Which painlessly no doubt she'd once had pierced –
All I do now, now flesh and symbol meet,
Is wonder if, to keep them free of pus,
She sponged with cotton wool swabs from a pleat
An antiseptic on her stigmata.

The duty officer at Calvary,
Who stood the closest to the prisoner's side,
Is reckoned by two gospels to have said,
'This was the Son of God', once Christ was dead.
So later if he heard without conviction
What else there was to Christianity
I hope he never thought the Crucifixion
Was when he'd just wished well of one who died.

ALEXANDER WILSON

My middle two names may make you laugh,
But I was christened to bury the dead,
I am the family cenotaph
For the younger brother my mother had.

He was the man in the photographs,
The smart lieutenant of the 12th Black Watch,
He was the ghost in the negatives
 Whose uniform haunted the dressing-up box.

Somewhere in Burma, freckled, red-haired
And hot in new khaki, he died in my stead.
Monsoons were his mourners, his epitaph mud.
By the time he was my age, he was seven years dead.

SISTER

Though neither of us ever stood
As straight as mother wished we would,
I stood up straight for, but I lost,
The brother-sister back to backs
Which mother refereed with books
And which I always hoped you'd lose,
You six-foot-tall hypotenuse.

Height was an issue less alive
When I was six and you were five,
Yet at a fancy dress parade,
Crawling behind you on all fours
I wished my mask has proper jaws
Because my wolf was not as good
As you, you smug Red Riding Hood.

And even when we went to school
We learnt no equalising rule,
Since your best subject was my worst
And you sat in and did for fun
The Maths that I was coached to learn.
So what made you turn Classicist,
Except that I had started first?

But then you won, to my disgrace,
The year I gained an Oxford place,
Your exhibition to St Anne's.
Though I resented you there more
After I'd found you in my room
Getting much further with a man
Than I'd got girls on that divan.

When people asked if we were twins
I matched our sallow, greasy skins,
Brown hair, brown eyes and lanky stance,
But now I wonder if they meant
Some symmetry of temperament,
Caused not so much by common genes
As competition in our teens.

So now I've got, while you have none,
A younger sister for my son,
I hope that they'll be different,
But let's hope, if they do compete,
They're sooner to admit defeat
Than both their father and their aunt,
Who haven't done so till they can't.

UNCERTAINTY

Graves of husbands, wives and lovers,
Like the churchyard manhole covers,
Proudly bear their maker's name,
But they're rotting all the same
When the earth the vicar blessed
And the turves have detumesced.

Whether you or I die first –
Can't think which I've most rehearsed –
Senseless fossil pollen grains
Will date our animal remains
To the first years grass grew flowers
Over either grave of ours.

But the knowledge I shall die
Cannot also tell me why,
Nor can all there ever is,
Nor all brief posterities
From Pre-Cambrian year dot
Till the universe is not.

HELEN

The rape of Helen and the sack of Troy
Began the odyssey of boarding school
With Latin bullying my mother tongue.
My sister, Helen, took a week to die,
My mother said, but I'd have been too young
To learn that in her backbone was a hole.
The bachelor Latin master who could cane
Taught the new Helen to a homesick boy.

And I imagined on the Trojan mound
A rampart crippled like a malformed spine
Round the cremated body of the town,
And when the Trojans saw the empty plain
Or Menelaus heard that she had gone,
Their legendary sorrows spoke for mine.

Hydrangeas test the soil's acidity.
The mirror triptychs in the bedroom windows
Collect the light in narcissistic pools.
Safe in their wellingtons and windcheaters
Peter and Jane are helping Daddy garden.
He clips the privet and they feed the bonfire.
Soon they will plant potatoes in its embers
And eat them, hard and gritty, after tea.
At dusk they listen to their bedtime story:
Henry the Green Engine who was immured
For disobedience like Antigone.

AUGUST AUTUMN

Ever since the news,
Your father has been obsessed
By individual trees
And the dying avenues
Which have caught Dutch elm disease.
Elms with jaundiced leaves
And stains of nicotine
Throughout the diocese
Are changing their natural green
To an August autumn brown;
And elms with no leaves at all
But rookeries scribbled among
The neat, botanically-drawn
Dead upper branches and twigs
Bring winter suddenly near.
These will have to come down
And quickly before they fall,
He says in his car beneath
With his father's walking stick
Beside the driving seat
As the only outward sign
Of the cancer in his lung
And the cancer in his spine.

At night when we go to bed,
My folded sweater prays
And my trousers genuflect
Over my bedroom chair
In attitudes of faith,
But the thoughts I try to collect
Until I drop off to sleep

Refuse to offer a prayer
To a hypothetical God.
Yet I will your father's escape
From a death of cancerous pain
And the dull uncomfortable ache
In his lower vertebrae
That wakes him or keeps him awake.
I have seen him preach to the mad
In a women's mental home,
Where he joined his hands to shape
An arrowhead on its way
To the heart of his Christian God,
And showed them how they could pray
The 'Our Father' like the sane.
But what will his God become
If the cancer attacks his brain?

As he gives you the wine or bread,
After I've watched him bless
Our son's oblivious head
Up at the altar steps
Where I have never knelt,
I read the hymnbook and wait.
But I find it nevertheless
Impossible now to forget
That your father's lifelong faith
Is an indirect result
Of an earlier painful death,
And that even Christ on the cross
In his foreign dead language screamed
A God-forsaken why
When the pain became too great.
Prayerbook and painkillers lie
On the seat of the bedside chair

By your father's side of the bed:
But oh how desolate, bare,
And unbelievably dead
Will a whole hinterland seem
To my own, I suppose, despair
When he and his certitude die.

REQUIEM

With crowded mourners and surpliced priests
Sit those who were once our wedding guests.

The stern archdeacon who married us
Offers the funeral address,

And where your father read our banns
Is an empty step where his coffin stands.

The same black fleet of cars on hire
Brought him and the bridal party here

And he found it difficult not to cry
As I do, biting back tears, today

At this sad marriage of love to grief,
This funeral of a married life.

He gave you away in ritual loss:
If he were here he could comfort us.

FIRE

It's company, she says,
As if the coal fire
Was a warm-hearted talker
From her part of Wales,
Or a genial smoker
Waiting for meals.

Each morning she stoops
And, setting aside
The blackened meshes,
Carries the still warm
Dust and ashes
Out of the widowed room.

EDDYSTONE LIGHT

for Debbie

On the horizon
On a clear day,
The Eddystone
Rivets sea to sky;
A midnight sun
On summer nights,
It strokes a zone
With northern lights.

But a gale warning
Crackling with static
Talks the storm in
From mid-Atlantic,
And waves come ramming
The outcrop of rock
Where light's informing
On depth and dark.

A wave breaks high
On the lighthouse stone,
The sparks of spray
Spatter to foam,
And if land and sea
Share Genesis weather,
Why shouldn't we
Who chose each other?

TWO DREAMS

In the first an adder,
One foot long and brown,
Basked on hill-fort pasture
Drought had done to a turn,
As I walked with my daughter
Around the dairy farm.

The other dream was odder:
I knew the woman's son;
I was his English master
And I had met her once.
Now we discussed her future
Over a buffet lunch.

The snake moved like a ripple.
I panicked for an axe
To sink into its middle –
A flash of blade and sparks
And head and tail would dribble
Writhing on dusty grass.

A Riesling stood on the table,
Lettuce and hard-boiled eggs.
The mother was suicidal:
Divorce was on the cards.
But as she peeled an apple
Had she made a pass?

My face in the shaving mirror
Is implicated still:
What Joseph said to Pharoah
Or Jung and Freud reveal
Can never root out my horror
Of the serpent or the girl.

THE OTHER WOMAN

'I thought you were the milkman.
I was going to pay next week.'
'Well, may I come in? It's freezing.
I've brought back Alan's book.'
I covet their central heating,
And the warmth of her physique.

Alan is out with the children,
And she tells me where. I know.
Moves as much as phrasing
Are all-important now.
She and I are sitting
Almost toe to toe.

Would I like some coffee?
If I say 'Afterwards, yes,'
At worst she can beg my pardon
Or smack me on the face.
The truth is that she whispers
'All I have on is my dress.'

But afterwards on the fluffy
Pelt of the fireside rug,
Should it be glowing carbon
Or lichen singed on a log
That I watch as she brings me slippers;
Then coffee stirred in a mug?

Framed photos of my children
Smile but cannot tell,
And so to save you guessing
I may as well reveal
That I dreamt up the setting
And most of its personnel.

Alan's book, the milkman,
Weren't they a give-away?
And such salacious treason,
It had to be a lie.
Or am I in her play-acting
An equally easy lay?

STAG

Behind iron railings,
To the rasping croup of his belling,
The harem huddles for bread,
Their black toes stuck in the mud,
Except for the doe he is following
Who will not lower her head
With that foghorn lowing and blowing
Vapours at each hindquarter
Of her already rain-licked fur.

She steps away, inches
Ahead of his antler branches,
Insisting the appetite
Grow and salivate
With the stir of her haunches.
And so they provoke and excite
Till she stops and he staunches
The open wound of her sex
With the brute force of his flesh.

STRUGGLE

A blackbird with split-nib bill
Open wide at an orange angle,

But the beak deformed and the bird dumb,
Strops the lower half on an earthworm.

The mauled intestine of the lawn
Oils a salad of dandelion.

As if excited by writhing meat
The blackbird works with an appetite.

Oh the suffering of them both!
Protracted hunger and slow death.

The worm that will never feel again
Topsoil juicy after rain,

The bird that will never know at all
Berries spherical in his bill,

The answerable mating-call.

HORSE

A horsebox parked by a Land Rover,
A blue saloon car with its hatchback open,
One sunlit afternoon in late October
In a paddock neither rural nor suburban.
A handsome pony with a thick blond mane
Is walked in circles past a group of men
Who might be bidding for the horse at auction.
But why the runny bloodstain on its groin?
Where is the foal if that's obstetric blood?
The small pink tube of a mollified erection
Is dangling like a teat and shakes its head,
Though why no mare if he is out to stud?
The wind strips beech trees for the coming winter.
I watch him led round, raw, domestic, neuter.

WATERSHED

The Bow River. Bow River.
Three men in his anecdote,
One with an artificial leg,
Were heading for rapids in a boat
On the Bow River. Or wherever.
Vague memories of lake and muskeg
In the Arctic Watershed
Looked for a Bow to rediscover.
Is that in Canada? I said.

Rocky Mountains. Banff, Alberta.
I know it, yes, and Lake Louise.
A girl, the current and a canoe
Are moving with me past dark trees
Once more into the unlived future
Fifteen or sixteen summers ago
One summer evening, almost night,
On cold coppery-green melt-water
Which I thought I would never forget.

ANOTHER COUNTRY

Sketched by a thirsty watercolourist,
Kids on hind legs, miniature black goats,
Begged an olive for its greenest shoots.
Hens pecked at their own shadows in the dust.
And a girl came, as if from a taverna,
Holding a perfumed, sugar-powdered cake
And a glittering beaker of stone-cooled retsina.
The young man thanked her, drank and ate.
Her questions were incomprehensible,
So on his pad he wrote in Attic Greek
With a Made in England 2B Venus pencil:
γραφω αλλα ου φημι – I write but do not speak –
And her amazement at the oracle
Flattered his manhood like the alcohol.

SOFT FRUIT

The strawberry leaves were autumn red
Nevertheless, nevertheless
In the straw of an empty bed
Where lightning whipped the frightened horse,
One late strawberry lay beneath
The fat warm teardrops of the rain,
A ruby on its hairy stem,
The eyeball of the horse insane
For shelter from the thunderstorm.

What was alive that I in fright
Took as the strawberry from the plant?
A snail was fattening on the fruit
While Miss Shapiro's tenor voice
The wet-nurse of an ammonite
Sang *Walking Back to Happiness*,
A cornucopia vivante
Indulging in a secret vice,
The client and the prostitute.

I divorce, be kind, be cruel,
Weeping berry, puckered foot
Pulled the mollusc from its meal
And by the misty Firth of Forth
Threw it in the undergrowth.
Fish and chips with tartare sauce,
Willow-herb and thistle-legs.
A train of inter-city thought
Crossed the cantilever bridge

Nevertheless, nevertheless,
Remembering the gutted snail
The berry parted from the mouth
Flesh retiring to the skull
And summer over in the North
Like Helen's teenage happiness
Which cost the fear inside the horse,
I could not bring myself to eat
The nibbled crimson of the fruit.

In the Jackdaw folder of 'Historical Genitalia',
The suitors of Elizabeth and reasons for their failure,
The Bonsai quality of Bonaparte's regalia,
What Hitler was missing in the region of Westphalia
Would all be investigated *inter* many *alia*.

Elizabeth I in a miniature by Hilliard
Scanned for masculinity by Hotson, Rowse and Tillyard,
The gusset of Napoleon expounded like the *Iliad*,
Hitler in his bunker playing pocket billiard
Would all be reproduced by the chiliad or milliard.

But if the young princess's *pudenda* were like Alice's
And only redetermined by Elizabethan malices,
If Bonaparte's was small because he owned huge palaces
And Hitler lost a ball when he gave the globe paralysis,
Do malicious jealousies provide all phallic fallacies?

PLEASURE

The only problem being where to begin
With such a bosomy buttocky physique:
To kiss, to nibble, bite or stroke the skin
Of downy suntan like a baby's cheek?

Fructified sunlight for pale northern flesh
To sink its apple-cleaned incisors in
Then wipe the fruit juice dripping from the chin.
The peach, *la pesca*, feminine, *la pêche*.

And taste the Mediterranean vitamin
Of one imported Common Market peach
More luscious than the slices in a tin,
Fresh peaches, blushing ripe and 10 pence each.

Even the peach-stone in the roof of the mouth
Would seem to fit the palate like a plate
Until the bow-point of the rowing boat
Needles the skin between the two front teeth.

Then suck the red meat from the wrinkled bone
Held to the life- and love-lines of the hand,
And dream how the kernel of this wooden brain,
If it were buried in its native land,
Could make a peach-tree come to life again.

NEAR ROUEN

If both Van Gogh and Nicolas de Staël
Could come in spirit back to France's soil
And spend a final exile in my soul,
I'd paint the arable hills of northern France

In August when the wheat is harvested,
The corn still listens to the scratch of crickets,
And maize a darker and unripened green
Holds in its leaves the cobs of heavier grain.

Cow-parsley on the verges of the D Road,
Straight kilometres of uneven tarmac
With dotted lines for gradients not bends
And telegraph-poles to emphasise perspective.

A wooded hillside on the skyline, sky
A blue misty with cirrostratus. Yes,
I think I'm thinking of the D1 or 2
Somewhere between Les Andelys and Ecouis,

A landscape framed in memory by the windscreen,
Not that I'd like to work or winter there
Or have the northern winter in my soul
That makes such harvests so desirable.

HOT WATER

The best bit of it, though, is getting in.
Hot water. Godliness. And naked skin.
So could this be the ultimate solution,
A dissolute dissolving in sensation,
A melting of both duty and desire
To a pure pleasure in the temperature?
The coloured abstracts and the full-length nude
Self-portrait, blameless in its self-regard,
The engine-room blood-noises of the brain
Relaxing underneath the water-line
Feel amniotic if not infinite.
Even the mini-whirlwind in the whirlpool
Gyrating at so many revs per minute
Repeats the planet's centripetal pull.

NIGHT-WATCH

While my father chanted 'Jamaica! Jamaica!'
In a poor imitation Caribbean accent,
During a televised 400 metre heat,
I explained aside to the agency nurse
That he was born in Jamaica. Nurse Marsh smiled
Politely, prettily, a newly-wed blonde,
Her watch-dial pinned like a campaign medal.
Two ambulance men manoeuvred the wheelchair

Out of the lift and next to the sick-bed.
One of them admired the balcony view:
Scots pine, grassy bank, mallow in flower.
The other crouched by the wooden fruit
Carved on the leg of the old hall table.
The phone rang often in the hot afternoon –
Offers to help from Beryl and Shirley.
The mind on the bed was drugged and wandered

To a childhood seaside holiday in Antrim.
Later we ate, three in the study,
Fried baby squid, mayonnaise, salad
And Riesling, followed by grapes and peaches.
Then we divided the night-watch between us.
I took till 4 and nodded off over
Mill on the Floss, Dodsons and Tullivers,
A Constable mill-wheel on the cover.

The next day the agency sent Jane Turner
Filling in time between Chepstow and Riyadh –
Jane who could name every one of the flowers,
Even love-in-a-mist and spiders-and-spoons

In the massive bouquet sent by the Centre.
My father showed me a scrap of confetti
Which fell from the pocket of the lightweight suit
Worn by Prince Charles to go away in.

My father intended to set the blue dot
As a paperweight in see-through plastic.
The Prince had spoken to my mother in her wheelchair
On what was her last appearance in public,
When he came to open the Bristol Centre.
And did I, walking to the car that evening,
Know it was the last time I had seen her?
Jamaica, Jamaica and love-in-a-mist.

CHERRY BLOSSOM BLACK

Kneeling like some strange four-footed beast
And cleaning my unfashionable shoes,
By which I mean elastic-sided boots,
On an old newspaper's forgotten news,
I dab the brush into the tin and try
Not to get any blacking on my suit,
Dark socks, white shirt cuffs, or the borrowed tie
As matt black as the polish on the boot.

The formal neck- and footwear of male grief
Serve as disguises for the funeral.
The tin and tin-lid, paper and still life
Are both a memory and memorial:
The sounds of shoeshine and the polish smell,
The putter-onner and the taker-off.

All stones look semi-precious on the beach,
If not to the fishermen in waterproofs
Or to the scatty Border Collie bitch
Racing below the sedimentary cliffs
Over the yeasty foam into the waves.
A balding man with full-sized bucket and spade
Is digging in the sand for lugworm bait.
One of the anglers, tired of hooking weed,
Catches a fish at last, a bass he says,
Long as his forearm and five pounds in weight,
Then folds the gasping metal of the fish
Into a rubbish sack to suffocate.
Rain smudges the horizon as I watch
A black sack flapping and the tide going out.

FLOWER SHOW

Would rose bushes exhibit if they could
Our sexual organs in a vase of blood?

A ROSE REPLIES

No, let it be said,
We plants are well-bred
And the thoughts of roses are pure.
We'd cut off your head
Before you were dead
And grind your bones for manure.

This is an equal opportunities statement.
Although it already has charitable status
And the rates on any building in which it is read
Are automatically zero-rated for a decade,
It seeks publicity no more than a test-tube foetus.

The recycled paper on which it is printed
Has been impregnated with potent microdots
Which when chewed are guaranteed to provide
A tasty meal of over 4,000 calories
With vitamins A to E for a family of four.

Scrumpled, it's a briquette of smokeless fuel
Which yields over three slow-burning megawatts.
The bottom left corner contains enough oestrogen
To be used as a fail-safe oral contraceptive.
Catholics may use it as a communion wafer.

It is all part of the ecumenical movement
And has been recognised by no less than the Pope,
The Kremlin, the White House and the EEC.
It has been approved by the silent majority,
And endorsed by such vocal minorities as

Christian Aid, The Basque Separatists
And the Variety Club of Great Britain, among many others.
It will end all wars, murder and masturbation.
It will annihilate disease and poverty.
It will eliminate all famines and droughts.

Like the Queen and her God of whose Anglican Church
    she is nominal head,
This document is officially of no political persuasion
And it does not carry any legal tender,
Though it may be the paper money of the future.
Anyone copying it by whatever means

Will be personally thanked. The film rights are free.
Correctly folded, it makes an origami Concorde,
Being a small but British contribution
To the freedom-fighters fighting for freedom
From oppression, pollution and over-population.

The letters in it are symbols of human endeavour,
And the white space around it stands for Antarctica,
The largest relatively unspoilt wilderness
On the planet misnamed Earth
Which should have been Ocean.

AND IN THE END?

Hardly have the primeval gases cooled,
Hardly has the volcanic magma boiled
When strange amoebae in the staring water
Die from the massive lack of oxygen.
The leafless conifers decay and fall.
Sea levels rise. The continents dissolve.
Tectonic plates and katabatic winds
Inherit the scorched surface of the earth.
The blood-red eyesore of a hotter sun
Tempers the igneous rocks to brick-kiln heat
In purple daylight full of sediment.
Weird sunsets haemorrhage in the stratosphere,
While rotting seaweed and dead shellfish smells
Linger for fifteen lunar months or more.
The polar ice-caps melt, till all the water
Evaporates in centrifugal fogs
Leaving the seabed as a glomerate
To harden in an airless atmosphere.
Hotplate by day, intensely cold by night,
The planet comes to emulate its moon:
No clouds, no rainfall, season, wind or sound.

Light-years away, in ignorance of this,
The stars are glinting in their dark address.

O

Sat and watched
full moon at moonrise
totally eclipsed
by a chimney stack.

Circular moonshine,
linear brickwork:
grandfather clock
time out of mind.

ON A LINE FROM CAVAFY

The hunter-gatherers settled into tribes,
Grew seeding grasses and fermented grapes,
Domesticated dogs and outlawed rapes,
Invented money and accepted bribes,
Decided they descended from the apes,
Told nationalistic jokes and published jibes,
Then watched their animal selves on videotapes.
Electric typewriters replaced the scribes
But no machine can free me from myself,
The luggage that I carry is the mind,
The mortal envelope is self-addressed
And there's no ship to take me from myself,
To liberate a soul so disinclined
Either to count his blessings or be blessed.

THE WAY THINGS ARE

The coffee shivers in concentric rings
And as the quayside seems to float inland
I walk on deck for sea-air and to watch
Weymouth become a postcard of itself,
Dorset a breakwater, the coastline cloud,
Our wake a ragged motorway of foam,
Where both a pigeon and a cabbage white
Are following the Red Ensign out to sea.

Back in the cafeteria-lounge, the youth
In Megadeth T-shirt and blue neckerchief,
The skull-and-crossbones buckle on his belt,
And reading Isaac Asimov is my son.
The girl with hiccups, sipping Diet Pepsi
And wearing a pink T-shirt, is my daughter.
Black cut-off jeans, blue watch-strap, pony-tail,
She's playing Guns N' Roses on a Walkman.

Rock muzak, rucksacks, Keep This Ship Tidy Bins,
Bermuda shorts, a Michael Jackson T-shirt,
A girl with ear-rings eating custard creams,
The mood is holiday and duty-free.
My wife is reading a Virago novel,
The Way Things Are by E. M. Delafield.
She's chewing Orbit sugar-free chewing-gum
But says she'd love 200 cigarettes.

Safety announcements in both French and English
Have spoken of emergency procedures,
Life-jackets, muster-stations, crew and drill,
A series of short blasts upon the whistle,
While I imagine what would happen if,
And in the daydream minutes before drowning
I play the hero and apologist
For love so long denied and ill-expressed.

RECENSION DAY

Unburn the boat, rebuild the bridge,
Reconsecrate the sacrilege,
Unspill the milk, decry the tears,
Turn back the clock, relive the years,
Replace the smoke inside the fire,
Unite fulfilment with desire,
Undo the done, gainsay the said,
Revitalise the buried dead,
Revoke the penalty and clause,
Reconstitute unwritten laws,
Repair the heart, untie the tongue,
Change faithless old to hopeful young,
Inure the body to disease
And help me to forget you please.

ULEY HOUSE

The flattened molehills stepping-stone the lawn
Towards fresh soil-heaps near the Judas tree.
Pink clematis flowers embrace a rusty cypress.
The creaking wingbeats of a wood pigeon
Applaud its exit from a copper beech
Into a sky of Pentecostal light
On a jasmine, bluebell, lilac-scented evening.
Rooks argue and a dog barks at a gunshot.
Among full moons of dandelion clocks
Heifers are tearing grasses in the sunset.
It's country life as *Country Life* would have it
And I'm so passive or dispassionate
I hear a desiccated holly leaf
Detach itself and fall through leaves to earth.

GIRONDE JULY

The wide and mud-brown tidal estuary
Was like the Mississippi, we imagined,
The ferry and its concrete landing-stage
A scene from the 1950s, we agreed,
Though river-crossing and the car-ferry
Already seem more than an hour behind.

It's 90 or a 100 in the shade;
The air outside's an oven like the car.
Dry ditches yellow with marsh marigolds
Go flickering by like vines and sunflower fields,
Though I am looking only for a bar
Which sells cold lager and iced lemonade.

We park behind a large Hôtel de Ville
Where providentially in a stone wall
We find a faucet labelled *eau potable*.
A push-button supplies it by the litre,
Splashes the feet and wets a ragged circle,
Flooding hands cupped to mouth with cold, clean water.

Meanwhile the tolling of a tinny bell
Is summoning to some ceremonial
The middle-aged of this provincial town,
All carrying their jackets for the heat.
A festival or saint's day? We can't tell,
Although there must be much to celebrate

Or so I think as we drive past the road-sign
And Mortagne, Mortagne-sur-Gironde,
Becomes a place to which I must return
If not in person sometime then in mind
As if the answer could again be found
In water reminiscent in the sun.

ON SUCH A NIGHT

We crossed the water by a duckboard bridge
A fraction above the river's darkened surface
And lay flat on our backs there on the beach.

Sand particles in our hair and stars above us,
Spectators of the galaxy we're part of,
We glimpsed the instant of a shooting star,

And touching on infinity and each other
I would have held your hand if such a séance
Could have redeemed ourselves and life together.

Instead we followed the shoreline past plantations
Of folded beach umbrellas in the sand,
Past seafood smells of sea and restaurant,

Towards the town, or where we thought the town was,
By walls and concrete blocks still hot to touch
As if the warmth could not escape till nightfall.

We heard the sea's night-noises feel for land,
Small waves collapsing into crevices
And interrupting fluent lights on water,

Till there it was: a place called Belvedere
Which I remember now for what it felt like
To be restored to what both feared forgotten.

NOT TESTED ON ANIMALS

Dear Andrew & Barbie, Many thanks.
Moroccan Rhassoul Mud Shampoo
For Hair Type: greasy with dry scalp!
How could you and how did you know?
A Body Shop shampoo which leaves
Moroccan grit grains in the bath
And looks like genuine sham poo.
Oh thank you, thank you, thank you both
And Happy New Hair to you too!

MR LARKIN

'This was Mr Larkin's style. It stayed
Consistent all his time with Faber, till
They lost him.' Disappointments, hopes that fade,
Pair up with minor failures of the will

To undeceive a gloomy poet chap,
Ironic, doubtful. 'Mr Larkin put
Contemporary verse back on the map.'
Death, boredom, fear and the iambic foot,

No trace of passion, violence or myth –
'I'll use it.' So it happens that I write
As Mr Larkin wrote, and tinker with
The same wry neo-Georgian stuff, and fight

By shrugging it all off as passing fad
The moderns A. Alvarez plugs as greats.
I know my Larkin: what he liked of trad.,
His preference for Hardy over Yeats,

Why he kept plodding on with form and rhyme –
Likewise his critic chums: Anthony Thwaite
Who praised him on the radio all the time,
And Amis who was quick to call him great.

But if he saw artistic suicide
Pre-empting the death to which his poems led,
And told himself that such was life, and sighed
And grumbled, without casting off the dread

That what we write defines our inner nature,
And at his age having no more to show
Than two good books should make him almost sure
He could have written better, who's to know?

(1977)

BIRCH

The charcoal rook
is a cancerous growth
in the blackened lung
of the winter birch,

an old lady
with Alzheimer's,
seventy, eighty,
unlearning the years.

The family silver
of bark and branches
is tarnished dark
and in need of a clean.

Bald and naked,
she has forgotten
the midsummer language
of green and leaves.

Sunsets electrify
her nervous system.
Storms mime grief
in a tragic display.

With a thirsty pain
under the earth,
her identical twin
seeks water, spring.

MEMORANDUM FOR THE GRAND PANJANDRUM

Administrivia are more and more a matter
Of total imbuggerance to me as an enemy
Of futile form-filling and carcinogenic jargon.
Who gives an acronym for idiotic idiom,
The turgid verbiage of oligarch's dittography,
The upstart footnote and its vermiform appendix,
Minutes of minutiae, quandaries of questionnaires,
Pleonastic paperwork, labyrinths of legalese
And photocopulation? Are you a fellow-sufferer
In post-potato Europe of pre-proforma trauma?
It's the Year of the Friend and I'm looking for a pen-friend.

CAT PEPPER WAR

I'd like to slap a writ upon
The cat that parked its situpon
Then sat and shat a pat upon
My daffodils and flattened them
Like date-palms lying shattered on
An atoll struck by atom bomb.

The dung has such a pungent smell
I know the perpetrator well:
Our neighbour's furtive Tortoiseshell.
I'll teach that brute to wipe her arse
On any of my blades of grass.
She'd better shift her features fast.

Cat pepper war! Drugged Kit-e-Kat!
Her days will be a living hell.
I'll make a scapegoat of that cat
And flay her for a welcome mat
Then nail her dead head in the hall:
The Bitch Bulb-basher of Bengal.

On second thoughts, or rather third,
I wonder what Herr Doktor Freud
Would think I'm trying to avoid,
Like Perseus mirroring the Gorgon,
By over-reacting to a turd,
A pussy and a yellow organ.

UNDERPASS

There is a tunnel leading to Heathrow
Which for pedestrians is a kind of hell.
I would not wish on foreigner or female
The journey down or back along that hole.

Beside a noisy four-lane motorway
The footpath leads for half a lonely mile
Towards a small low-wattage bulb of daylight.
Graffiti. Dirt. Exhaust fumes. Diesel fuel.

The heart-beat is a bird stuck in an oil-slick
But there's no other way except this ill-lit
Bleak corridor next to the cycle-track,
The air monoxide and polluted concrete.

And there's your shadow lurking with a flick-knife.
If days resembled fiction or a film,
This tunnel's where I would be mugged or murdered.
'Your passport and your wallet or your life!'

It's less than true that what we fear is fear.
We're frightened of our cowardice and the truth:
That there are earthbound souls who never soar
And want revenges for their mis-spent youth.

IN THE UNDERWORLD

Clockwatchers stare at advertising space
Where Pornutopia meets with paradise
And promised lands of vines and lingerie
Ransom their happiness at purchase price.

There is a beggar man at Waterloo,
At Piccadilly needles and syringe.
At Oxford Circus a fly-posted booth
Is advertising what the flesh will do.

The poster of a famous opera star
Has pupils made of tooth-marked chewing-gum
Which blinds his eyes and Frankensteins his stare.
A smear of curry sauce has smudged him dumb.

With his guitar-case for a begging-bowl
A student haunts a subterranean song.
A carborundum spark of stainless steel
Lights up the tunnel like a smoker's lung.

This is both human sewer and London Zoo.
Each mica grain inside its metal stair
Glitters as steely as a distant star.
We are the souls in Purgatorio.

ANNO DOMINI

Beyond both Alnmouth and the Aln,
Above a boat-filled estuary,
A cross stands on a mound or dune
Like a cathedral drowned in sand,
A small hill for a Calvary
Up which a figure in the sun
Climbs to the top, then kneels in prayer,
As if she were illusory,
A pilgrim from an earlier age
Or apparition on a screen,
Dressed in the habit of a nun.

But kneeling there she joins her hands,
Bows to the cross to meditate,
Then wanders to the water's edge,
Takes off her shoes and cools her feet
Where North Sea meets Northumberland.

And we that evening walk around
The saltmarsh, as the sun goes down,
To find the ruins of a shrine
With Saxon carvings on the arch.
We take a sandpath up the mound
To touch the upright of the cross
And read the letters round the base:
St Cuthbert A.D. and a date,
A founding father of the church
Whose landfall it commemorates
In silent stone above a beach.

Above the beach in silent stone,
The halo of a harvest moon
Illuminates the planet's rim
And worshipping the setting sun
The tidal waters seem to flame.

BRINKBURN PRIORY

A doorway through a Norman arch.
Whispers echo at the silence,
Eyes adjusting to the dark
In cellar smells of ancient stonework
Void of worshippers and pews.
Sunlight through the stained-glass windows
Glazes terracotta tiles.
A bird is flying in the rafters.
Wildflowers drying on the altar
Are ragwort, knapweed, willowherb.

The Risen Christ by Fenwick Lawson,
Born in 1932,
Dominates the northern transept:
Displaying hands in benediction,
A giant airborne monk in beechwood
Hangs aloof on chains and metal.
Strange to find the resurrection
Signified by weight of wood:
Apotheosis of a tree-trunk
Posing as a rib of God.

Two girls are playing in the garden
With a length of fraying rope,
Moles have undermined the lawn,
Rosebay willowherb in sunlight
Seeds along the riverbank;
The water, noisy as a torrent,
Carves its channel out of sight.
Beech trees dominate the valley
Witnessing a prehistoric
Resurrection into leaf.

FAIR COPY

*On being asked for two poems in manuscript to be exhibited
in the new library of his old school.*

Which of my voices should I choose
To represent me and my views?
The quizzical aimed to perplex?
The puerile obsessed with sex
So both cold frames may gather dust
Round manifestos of dry lust?

Which of my faces shall I wear?
Morose, profane, or debonair?
Should I parade a wound or bruise
For generations to peruse
On library shelves behind a book
As at their mirrored selves they look?

The mystic or the moralist?
The joker or the journalist?
Or sheepish wolf in shepherd's clothing
In love with self and/or self-loathing?
What have I got to gain or hide
From specimens beneath a slide?

After a period of neglect,
My vanity and intellect
Prevaricate and then rejoice
In the dilemmas of the choice.
It is an honour. I accept,
Evasive, humble, proud, inept.

But what if I have not fulfilled
The artistry a schoolboy willed?
What if I have, through failure, failed
With hopes abandoned, faith curtailed,
To ratify the work begun
With one thing to perfection done?

There. It is better said and out;
There is more certainty in doubt
And future perfect time will tell
Whether or what is written well
And if the language lives or dies
With all that it exemplifies.

Words to the living to be read,
These are the poems I have shed,
So let them be a floral wreath
And countersignature to death:
Long live life as long as art
Can liberate the human heart.

LA BREA

I am the tarred and feathered stork
Who flapped its limbs until they stuck.

I am a tapir ancestor
Who came for water, swallowed tar.

This is the asphalt killing-ground,
A lake that thirsts. Beware. Be warned.

His trunk a blowhole out of reach,
A mammoth trumpets liquid pitch.

We are a pack of dire wolves
Who scented death and mired ourselves.

I am the grief of a giant sloth
Who drank the waters of black death.

Lion and lioness salivate
At bison ready trapped to eat.

Coyote, jaguar and puma
Die for a taste of dying llama.

A squirrel bleating in distress
Allures a rattlesnake to death.

The tar immobilizes both
The short-faced bear and sabretooth.

The water winnows skeletons
Caught in a trap of sun and rain.

I am the skull of the only human,
Anonymous La Brea Woman.

The sump of ancient swamp-remains
Swallows the battles of old bones.

The eagle and the condor drown
In liquid nightfall underground.

SEVERN BORE

Flowing muddily through the meadows
Past orchards, cows and banks of clay,
Past shivering trees' inverted shadows,
The Severn broadens on its way.

Funnelled as if towards a sluice,
Bara, a billow from Old Norse,
Spreads rapidly across the Noose
Its equinoctial tidal force.

A noisy train at Minsterworth,
It rounds the corner with a swerve,
A wall of water and a wave
Drenching the willows with brown surf.

Shipping the driftwood back upstream
With smells of estuary and reeds,
It fills the channel like a reen
And still the water levels rise

As if it ran away from sea
And half the ocean were to come
Collapsing on the valley trees
In a catastrophe of foam.

And there look up! The daylight moon
Oblivious to all these words
Floats like the North Atlantic's brain
And floods a river in reverse.

NEW YEAR'S EVE

On this, the last day of the year,
that now inseparable pair
like crescent moon and evening star,
both metal-bright and crystal-clear
against a blue crepuscular,
enact their dance of near and far
prehistories of the calendar
before they seem to disappear,
a sickle and a nymphaea,
into the cold December air.

MISERY

I've caught the train to Misery.
I know each stop and station:
Regret, Remorse and Jealousy,
Revenge and Resignation.

There's no escape across the sea:
An airline takes you there.
The pilot is despondency,
The passenger despair.

JOB DESCRIPTION

Dogsbody. Despot. Saint and martyr.
Diplomat. Bureaucrat. Creep and tartar.
Tamer of lions, cobra-charmer.
Nuclear warhead and disarmer.
Expert with parents, sons and daughters,
Weasel words and troubled waters.
Menagerie manager/manageress,
A human dynamo hooked on stress.
An innovative facilitator,
Proactive professional loyalist traitor.
Workaholic with sense of balance,
Renaissance figure with multi-talents,
Gravitas and a winning smile,
Impeccable manners and perfect style.
A drudge, a drone, a worker ant,
A meek impoverished sycophant
Who craves acceptance and admittance,
Suffers fools gladly, works for a pittance.
Name two referees, one of them God.
No weirdos please. Apply in blood.

ALEC

Throned in a wheelchair, mouth open, being fed
In paralytic second babyhood,
I smile and wink but leave the rest unsaid.
I know I'm talking scribble parrot-phrase
As words unravel in my addled head,
A tower of Babel in the Blitz ablaze.
Dementia has demeaned me and diminished
All memories of anyone I cherished.
(Who is that woman? Did I marry her?)
Deteriorating synapses have perished
All the co-ordinates of love and care.
Each day now is a sentence left unfinished.

FATHER

The skeleton in its shroud
and the skin on the head so cold,
the teeth in the mouth half open
as if to yawn or laugh,
and nose stuck in the air,
the death-mask stare of the eyes,
and typical wisps of hair
over the stone-cold scalp,
with a grandpaternal look
in a pose of imagined repose
under two paintings of yours,
The Roofs and *Coverack*
both from your palette-knife phase,
with two of your purchases:
the hunting esquimaux,
two huntsmen in canoes,
pursuing caribou
swimming white Arctic seas
and the land-hunt on the snow
in turquoise, pink and blue.

And so the memories stir
elsewhere in other time
of selves in another year
and I imagine you now,
a big man in your prime,
consultant and physician,
who would have ministered
to the old man in the bed
with quadriplegia,
dementia or whatever,
till he becomes once more

the handsome sporting hero
double-blue thwarted by war,
the Greyhound No 8
and freshman Magdalen oar.

The marriage to Norah Wilson,
the young Paulina girl
next door at Lexham Gardens
who tackled the arrogant chap
walking each day to St Paul's
in a tasselled rugby cap.

The Hausa Grammar, foxed
from his days as the 'plausible Major'
with the West Africa Corps
in Northern Nigeria till
bilharzia saved the doctor
from Burma and the war.

The conjurer who could
with a copper penny seem
to rub it behind his head,
then, with revolting mime
and hideous snorting noise,
forehead purple with strain,
sneeze through his hairy nose
the same unbloodied coin
with George VI who died
and Rule Britannia waves.

The wacky, eccentric don
who collected the works of Jung,

The Tibetan Book of the Dead,
Ouspensky and Gurdjieff,
a theosopher who read
Meister Eckhart and Freud,
Boehme and Swedenborg,
Lilliput and Dan Dare
in the Eagle before I did.

I could not now rehearse
those arguments we had,
philosophical battles,
typical son and dad
antler-locking rebuttals
of youth by adulthood
or was it the reverse:
the dogmatism of youth
and sceptical adult pride
locked in empirical proof?

The paterfamilias
at his most generous self
dispensing food and drink,
glass after excellent glass
of vintage Bordeaux wine
kept to its perfect time,
decanted with fuss and finesse
and warmed to an optimum.
Here's to our very good health
and bottle-filled cellar-shrine.

He who endowed me with life
looks like Brueghel's Aveugle
with his mouth half open to laugh
and his eyes' unseeing gaze.
The shape of the skull and the scalp

and the skull-cap cranium
round the brain which once contained
the names of every bone
in the body which lies so still
in rigor mortis repose.

I kiss the forehead farewell,
cold as a statue now,
the scalp and the cheeks are cool
and lifeless as the snow
or the huntsmen in canoes
pursuing caribou
across the Arctic seas
in turquoise, pink and blue.
So rare for the end to be
triumphant like the start,
So rare for the head to obey
the dictates of the heart.
Father, forgive, I pray.
Be near me now we part.

ENIGMA

In a basilica of air,
An ancient moon of sun-baked clay,
A terracotta text inscribed
Like flat earth and the turning globe,
Stares out at us with one blind eye.

Discovered in a mud-brick chest,
A cryptogram of hieroglyphs
In spirals on a two-faced disc
Thwarts scholar and philologist
With its elusive mysteries.

Revolve the symbols in the mind:
A goatskin rug and shield embossed,
Upstanding fish, farm implements,
A flower in blossom, grain and plants,
The crested head and walking man.

Retrace the spiral of the signs
From centre to circumference
And back again as in a dance.
Is it the lyric of a song,
A hymnal or a game of chance?

A walking man reads left to right
A series of dumb images
Surmising melodies for flute
Before the feathered myths took flight
And Christians realigned the fish.

Why do I look so long and hard
Almost with love and reverence
At these beginnings of the word,
While indecipherable stars
Assume their insignificance?

SUB-MINOAN

The most beautiful
piece in the Archaeological
Museum is not
the bull's head
libation cup
in black steatite
nor the ivory acrobat,
the snake goddess,
octopus ceramics,
nor gold bee pendant,
though they are miracles
of creation, craftsmanship,
loss and retrieval,
but the young attendant
in Gallery XII,
poised on her chair
between pithoi
and sarcophagi.

ECLIPSE

To celebrate their fire-on-stone
Anthropomorphic nuptial fling,
She wears a hole-in-one-club brooch
And non-existent diamond ring
With lunar valley necklace pearls
And golden bracelet round the bone
As tidal waters on the beach
Are agitated into foam.

While coronation of the moon
With crown of flames and ring of fire
Enacts a pageant of rebirth,
The sun becomes a crescent moon,
A furnace door of flaming mouth
Ingests a mandala of stone
And sun and moon are making love
Or so it seems from darkened earth.

As if it were a passing phase,
The sun emerges to ignite
The chemistry of genesis
On fields of gravity and light's
Historic choreographies
And then they go their separate ways,
The sun-god and the satellite,
Innumerable nights and days.

DRAGONFLY

With wings of tissue-paper quartz
it dragonflies and dragonflits,

a bullet of metallic sheen,
a flying samurai machine,

a humming-bird on skimming flights,
then like a butterfly alights

and leans to drink from lily pads
libations offered to the gods,

a lace-winged ephemopteron
whose turquoise jewelled abdomen,

a photon of the worshipped sun,
shines iridescent and is gone.

COMBING THE BEACH

A stone, abraded and round,
pitted and white like the moon,

another the shape and size
of an almond sugared white,

a fragment of shell as smooth
and enamelled as a tooth,

hinge of a mussel shell
glinting with mother-of-pearl,

a broken nugget of quartz
scintillating with sparks,

slate in a tiny flake
and a piebald pebble for luck,

a shard of striated shell
still with a seafood smell,

a mollusc's auricular curve
echoing distant surf,

and a globe of luminous stone –
hold it towards the sun,

read the translucent veins
or lick the salt from the lens

to polish the colours afresh
before they evaporate

like life from the eye of a fish.

BOUGAINVILLAEA

Why desire
to preserve forever
purple bougainvillaea
over turquoise sea,
not that the bluey-green
reflective aquamarine
is exactly turquoise
nor the balustrade of violet
purple in fact
or cobalt violet
and not flowers but bracts
over delicate florets
against a sunlit sea,
itself a fractured fluid
mirror of the sky's
nonentity?
Purple, mauve, violet,
it depends on the light
and idiolect
of the individual
viewing leaves as flowers
and, as Goethe
is said to have said,
even a sensitive person
can only look
at the sunset
for a limited time
or words to that effect.

Sounds like a hornet or a wasp.
How can I tempt it to escape?
What does it see in a bathroom light
And lampshade with its star designs?
A sunflower stamen of hot moon
To energise and pollinate?

With rolled-up cosh of magazine
I try to lift the creature free.
It buzzes to the shade again
And hits the lightbulb with a ding.
Blinded by after-images
I stun it to the ground in fright

And glad it cannot testify
I club the living daylights out.
So was it just a hover fly
Or *volucella bombylans*,
A mimic of the bumble bee?
A samurai with Christian wings,

It had a bumble bee's low drone
And yellow with black tiger stripes
Its markings simulated wasp.
I hold it up to magnify
The Giant's Causeway of its eyes'
Bronze eyeballs in the stiffened corpse,

Dry, lightweight now. My breath can move
What seemed electric when alive.
In death so fragile it was love.

BEACHED

Like ancestors we decorate our caves
with images to make us feel at home.
The Chinese whispers of the little waves
issue their own obituaries in foam.

The powdered rock, the salt solution, air
where fronds and feather shapes of nebulous ice
on sunlit sky which is not anywhere
remind the writer nothing happens twice,

as through the hour-glass of each idle fist
I run the warm particulates of sand.
Time is a millstone and the body grist
to molecules of water, sky and land.

But where's the rationale, the *raison d'être*,
Our universe has this or any feature?
Why do we lie here beached like injured creatures
unready to evolve into the future?

MEMENTO

Bearded Poseidon on the mantlepiece,
A photo of her father, Captain Mann,
Whose second daughter was Elizabeth,
The Universal Aunt to family,
Miss E. D. Mann, the grown-up who could play
Blow-football with us and Monopoly.

Great Auntie Betty showed us how to conjure
Brown woollen pompoms out of cardboard circles
And hollow swans from flattened silver paper,
Made holly berries out of sealing wax,
Taught us Clock Patience and then Spite and Malice,
Smoked Kensitas and harvested the coupons.

We loved her stories and her childish laughter:
'We gave him mousetrap cheese instead of soap.
He scrubbed and scrubbed and still it wouldn't lather.'
Outback on evenings in Australia,
She'd learnt to smoke to fumigate mosquitoes.
Her hoopla'd smoke rings wobbled like a signal.

Now when I think of Auntie B I hear
The bleeping of a deaf-aid maladjusted,
The clinking shopping bags of Cyprus sherry,
I see a dogged hook-nosed hen in glasses
And endless games of two-pack patience stalled
In feudal columns on a wooden tray.

She wrote my name in loopy handwriting
And added for inscription on the card:
'My badge worn all through First World War in France
Queen Alexandra's Imperial Nursing Sisters'
And safety-pinned the ribbon to the paper.
I keep the keepsake like a talisman.

The flat. The room. The nursing home. The coffin.
The girl. The nurse. The aunt. The Great Aunt Betty
Who has no bronze memorial but this.
I see you arriving somewhere on a ship
Met at a quayside by the bearded man.
It is an anchorage and you embrace.

OPEN 365 DAYS

With a cough of steam
it seems to come
almost on time

from its under-
ground chamber
smelling of sulphur,

a sudden eruption
from souterrain
onto the scene,

a nebulous feather
of hot white water
and steam under pressure,

both genie and ghost,
a hothouse growth
of miraculous birth

for less than a minute
splashes the intimate
flesh of the planet

until it relapses
onto the plateaux
of its own applause.

On bamboo and grass
hot droplets glitter
like dew or stars.

PETRIFIED FOREST

Next to a living stand of Douglas Fir,
We touch the redwood like an ancestor.

It is a sculpture in its sepulchre.
The clothes of resurrection do not stir.

A BETTER BERRY

'Doubtless God could have made a better berry,
but doubtless God never did.'
Dr Boteler quoted by Izaak Walton

Reach down between the green serrated groves
And feel for berries' ripened crimson selves
Wearing their seeds like buttons on a sofa,

Twiddle the six-point star of Bethlehem
Between your pink forefinger and your thumb
To reinvent the wheel with leaf and stem,

Then with some Amaretto – just a splash –
Taste at its best, sun-ripened and picked fresh,
The veiny brainwork of the sweetened flesh

With caster sugar crystals by the spoonful
And cream poured in a languid waterfall
Onto the waiting strawberries in a bowl,

Then savour both the shape in the saliva
And that infallible midsummer flavour
As if you were in love and it your lover,

Moving the proof from lips to uvula
And swallow, swallow till the fever's over,
As if in heaven and an unbeliever.

INSOMNIA

Your mentors and tormentors join
in the small hours to toss a coin
the coin is you and heads or tails
whichever choice it always fails
call for the bottle narcotize
with television sex food lies
another addled egghead cracked
inside the factory of fact
where dawn attacks with blacks and blues
the sunset is a psychic bruise
and night and day land sky and sea
are solipsists like you and me
so sleep on it and wake up worse
call for a psychiatric nurse
delete the fate you cannot face
also-ran in a one-horse race
and what you have is what you've got
from cancer ward to carrycot
but what is that you nenuphar
floating lily or drowning star
it's all too little and too late
to hibernate or aestivate
so scrub the future shred the past
as overcrowded overcast
if things are never what they seem
it's only an anxiety dream

VISION MIXER

Abracadabra. Magic wand.
Please read my thought-waves and respond.

You know my number. Ring me now.
Surprise yourself and break a vow.

Distressed, possessed, *id est* obsessed,
I have this passionate request.

I want you now. I want you here.
I want you in my egosphere.

I'm willing you to drive this way.
Telepathy. I hope and pray.

Drop everything. Get in the car.
Accelerate. Come as you are.

Without you time goes oh so slow
Today began ten years ago.

The calendar's a vacant show,
Its state of mind is status quo.

The sky is dark, the answer's no,
The small hours are the longest though,

North of despair and east of woe
Where autumn thinks of winter snow.

Tonight began more years ago
Than I would ever let you know.

ZOOLOGICAL GARDENS

Anti-clockwise round and round
the oval concrete pond,
he paces with both eyes half-closed,
ears flapping back and forwards with each step.
The tubular prehensile snout
uncurls to sniff and suck between
the giant toenails of his round front feet.

She meanwhile strips a branch of leaves
and lunches off them.
She's swaying rhythmically
as if she had in mind
some melody or dance.

He snorts a scoop of gravel
and spray-dusts his back,
picks up an apple bobbing green in water
and places it inside his whiskered mouth
between discoloured and uneven tusks.

Shifting methodically from foot to foot,
she pulls and chews more greenery.

And as he passes on his rounds,
the trunk sniff-feels for her until
another large proboscis gradually appears.
The human adults joke and snigger as,
preoccupied and ponderous, he paces round,
a naked prisoner at exercise,
then tries to mount her, fails, and tries again.
Men, women, children gather, shouting, laughing,
a circus crowd as for a circus act:
two Asian elephants in Melbourne Zoo.

She turns and raises by its muscled root
her fly-whisk tail,
and slowly, gently wades into the water
until knee-deep
to help him mount and couple with her,
though not for long, and afterwards,
protuberance retreating into pouch,
the bull continues on his rounds again.
Impassively, she turns her back on us
and briskly drops
three neatly-formed and ochre turds
into the drinking water where they float
and then she urinates
to human protestations of disgust
as if instinctual desires writ large
were both inhuman and preposterous.

TARGET

When I was on my way to teach
One Saturday in shirt-sleeve order,
A pigeon in a copper beech
Admiring a herbaceous border,
A bottom-heavy type of bird,
A winged and feathered tub of lard
With an intestinal disorder,
Released a liquid pigeon turd.

What had it eaten? Dread to think.
What puddles had it had to drink?
At least it missed the balding head
And hit the shoulder blade instead,
Thus staining shirt of Virgin blue
With guano splat of pigeon poo,
An epaulette of khaki-white
And evil-smelling pigeon-shite.

So shirtily that Saturday,
'I have been shat upon,' I say.
The swollen yahoo of a bird
Less gastroenteritic turd
Feels meanwhile lightened of its load
And like a levitating toad
It takes off through the branches to
A sky of unsuspecting blue.

PARC LIAIS

Between the port and esplanade,
A granite head commemorates
The naturalist-astronomer,
Emmanuel Liais, former mayor,
With an oasis off the street,
A garden full of tropic trees,
A hothouse of exotic flowers
And, in the grove beyond the lawn,
An ornamental lily pond
In which a central fountain plays.

It is a place where lovers come
To talk and hold each other's hands,
A centrepiece for pensioners,
For friends and midday picnickers
Who choose a seat in sun or shade
And contemplate the play of light
Around the pear-shaped lily pond
Or watch the fountain's plumage change
And hear it imitating rain
While it is glittering in the sun.

So purposefully and in vain
The water droplets rise and pause
In fluctuations of the breeze,
Then fall obedient to the law
Of gravity's near-perfect aim,
Its own musician and applause,
Since water as no artist can
Reciprocates a flawless sky,
Quenches the thirst and can become
The tears and humours of the eye.

SONG

dear friend
much missed
long time
no see
let's end
this fast
while I'm
still me

no time
like now
while we
exist
to sow
the seeds
get pissed
and how

in end
no sea
no time
so long
no me
no friend
no wine
no song

A poem
written
in blood
or bone
is not
forgotten
nor alone

in sweat
of art
and hurt
of years
words are wet
with blood
and tears

A poem
learnt
by heart
or hurt
is burnt
for comfort
in the night

and though
the makers
die and go
what the letters
say and do
can console us
dying so

console
atone
and entertain
the soul
in pain
and make us
whole.

CLIMBING MY FATHER

The egg-timer releases upside down
A fraying thread of rusty-coloured sand.
We're in the kitchen underneath the clothes rack
Hung with Sea Island Cotton underpants
Which seem gigantic, he a giant too.
Hands in his helping hands, feet on his knees,
I clamber up the stomach muscles' wall,
Cross wobbly areas of wincing flesh
Up to his chest, fling legs across his shoulders,
Until eureka I am looking down
On fluffy hair and suntan on the summit.
The clothes rack on a pulley now in reach,
He lowers me from ceiling to the ground.
The eggs are boiled. And mountains washed to sand.

SECOND CHILDHOOD

He's grown a beard and looks like Jeremiah
In his pyjamas but as biddable
As a young child or more so, to be fair.
Though much of what he says is verbal scribble,
He can respond to music and old friends
But can't remember where his radio is
Or how to switch it on and tune the dial.
He walks with the assistance of a stick
And often answers 'don't know' or pretends.
His medic's memory, once formidable,
Has disappeared into the brain's abyss.
Of all the things I showed him on our walk,
He liked the spring lambs best: white herbivores
Practising vertical take-off on all fours.

80

It is his birthday and the two old men
embrace and hug, their cheeks not touching, then
they part and hold each other, looking into eyes
octogenarian and young again
as if at the imponderable surprise
that they should be empirically alive
towards the end of their own lifetimes.

'My dear old friend,' says Peter weighing words
which Alec now can only smile towards.
They touch and it is touching, move and moving.
Contemporaries at school and college friends,
both are more sentimental now and loving
as if they held the present of each other
against their non-existence altogether.

DEAR JOHN

John Henry Franklin Eminson
(1956–1998)

I remember the pints of beer,
your acumen and fluent pen,
your civil servant's admin mind,
mental arithmetic no fear,
faster than a calculator,
your terrier-like tenacity,
the Billy Bremner of a team,
your dress-sense and the man-made fibres,
your unswerving loyal support
of losing and lost causes like
Doncaster Rovers (never say die),
your justice and integrity,
a right-hand man in bunker days,
your boyishly paternal pride
in Mark and Charlotte, then in Tom,
and your judicious words of praise,
your love of literature and sport,
the population of each novel,
the poet's personalities
and the inhabitants of plays
since it was people who make days
for the would-be football journalist
who married in his Oxford phase,
protective of the underdog,
the misfit's mentor with a true
relish of individuals –
why has it taken me so long
to choose these words to say of you?

Because of all those troubled years?
The ailing mother in a home,
the marriage moving to divorce,
the mind not stable and the grim
'Duncan, you do not understand
how truly desolate it is,
the blankness of a blank despair',
the therapy ('she has your eyes')
and loneliness which drink disguised.
What chemical imbalance or
disturbance of a troubled mind
led you one morning and your car
to the hard shoulder out to find
a death which could not swerve in time?
It was unlike your better self
to bother someone else and leave
a family of four to grieve.

Agnostically, I hope you saw
the chapel full of people who
loved you for what you meant and were
and in that coffin as you lay
or else inanimate at last
I wish your troubled spirit rest.
And I remember one good friend
say in the crematorium
that anyone who really knew
could never fail to love you too.
We could not understand both why
and how it was you had to die.
I speak as if you still exist
and you could listen to me try.
Ah well, dear John, you always were
a sympathetic listener.

THEOCRACY

O Dad of donnée, data, all that's given,
Your majesty, our feudal lord in heaven,
Your wish is our command both here and there.

Give us our daily modicum of food
And do not take us to the moral cleaners
For major or for minor misdemeanours,
As we forgive those who forget a feud.

Please don't seduce us with temptation's dare
But keep us on the narrow straight and level,
With no remission for a devious devil.

Omnipotence and glory hallelujah
Are yours as long as always has a future,
Since you're the boss, King God, the grand panjandrum
Of random balls. *Quod erat demonstrandum.*

DO YOU WANT TO PUT GOD IN THE RECYCLE BIN?

right mister right mister right mister right.
dear god of particle acceleration
and landlord of infinity and night
inventor of equations and creation
engenderer of gender differences
the artist-dreamer and supreme creator
of superstrings and other galaxies,
dear astrophysical predestinator,
have you a website and dot com address?
What search engine would open up your portals?
How can a hacker calculate or guess?
Please listen sometimes though we are mere mortals.
We aren't all einsteins newtons aristotles
but dodos sending messages in bottles

A DICTIONARY OF WALKING MISQUOTATIONS

There is more enterprise in walking naked
Though life is not a stroll across a field;
You cannot fertilize it with a fart.
Tears, idle tears, I know not if they mean
The course of true love never did run smooth.
Sunt lacrimae rerum. You have to laugh.
Hope springs eternal in the human breast
But there's no ship to take me from myself,
Time will say nothing but I told you so
To justify the ways of God to man
Or vice versa – all is relative,
Reality can't bear much humankind
But *Eli, Eli, lama sabachthani*
And so say all of us. The rest is silence.

BLACKBIRD AT DUSK

Visible only as orange beak
and not so much for its dark physique,
a blackbird sits in a sycamore tree
and sings what it's like for him to be.

It sings of earth and sings of sky,
of water's depth and the fiery eye,
it sings for life and the love of leaves
as words rejoice and music grieves.

MUTE SWAN

Treading an arrogant V in water,
I look at myself and my own image:
eye to eye with an orange beak,
a bird with aristocratic hauteur,
a beautiful and cantankerous face
on a pure white body and snake-like neck.
Preening myself, I drink the mirage
and its embodiment of grace.

I too can walk on water as I run
beating my widespread wingspan down the lake,
until on gentler currents I am airborne.
The Holy Ghost may double as a dove
but I am more immaculate as a swan
and I too am a god when I make love.

WASP

Where the hell's the fucking exit
from this bloody box of gloom?
seems to say the angry insect
in its waspish idiom.
Sees the light and then attacks it,
savagely monotonous.
Light behind the window tricks it
to reiterate its loss.
A timid biped tries to coax it
into freedom out of doom,
with a paper guides and pokes it,
death-wish flying round the room.
Climbs the malice of the glazing
in a fury of despair,
tiger-stripes of anger blazing,
entrance equals . . . *Exit*. Zoom!
Freedom. Independence. Air

MINUTES

The minutes of the previous meeting
in lumpy pedestrian prose
were appraised and approved by bleating,
matters arising arose,

and the items on the agenda
verbosely came and went:
compromise fought surrender;
meaning clarified meant.

Is there any other business?
A whole lot more, he thought.
Why should we act like prisoners
when time is far too short?

We are free to use our talents.
We shall all too soon be dead.
Let's live and to hell with balance.
Shall we minute that? they said.

Let's all get wasted this minute.
Let's party into the night.
And as for the paperwork, bin it.
It's trivial trouble and trite.

Now is for loving and laughter,
Let fluids in friendship flow.
The minutes of matings hereafter
Are over wherever we go.

DECENT CITIZEN

It's so damn awkward being British
Although my passport says I am,
Born Oxford, 1947.
Well, maybe I am Anglo-Scottish.
How do I seem to you, my man?
So sorry. Ladies, gentlemen.
A vaguely bookish, Rupert Brookeish
Anachronistic English gent
Safe beneath his English heaven
Of fashionably mixed descent,
Urbane, ironic, wry and skittish?
Or another inhibited Englishman
Inhabited by a Caliban
Who wished he didn't give a damn?

THEORY

In our Greco-Roman youth
We believed in love and truth.
In post-modernist decline
Signifier questions sign.

TOMORROW

From the beginning of the day
when sunrise shoots its arrow
until the remnants of the sky
in darkened charcoal narrow,
what is there left for me to say
in anger or in sorrow
and what's the purpose of today
if not to be tomorrow?

I talk myself to sleep at night
or cry into my pillow.
The world outside is cancelled light
and shadows lying fallow.
Why did you have to go away,
was there no time to borrow
and what's the purpose of today
or reason for tomorrow?

Though reassuring clichés say
that better times will follow,
tomorrow is another day
whose promises are hollow.
If you were god to you I'd pray
in anger and in sorrow
to give us back our yesterday
and recreate tomorrow.

ALL SAINTS

A cold wind from the east
blew seagulls inland
to where Canada geese
cornered the foreground
in front of the island,
Isleworth Ait,
where a heron landed
among leafless willows,
the mud-brown Thames
washed its tidal foreshore
and the cold east wind
dishevelled the water.

The mourners foregathered
by the Saxon tower
and the modern nave
of All Saints' Church.
Young men looked older,
thickened, hair thinning.
Relatives arrived
in sombre dark clothing,
recognised, spoke,
spoke of the sadness,
registered shock
while popular music
played his favourite songs.

Just after eleven
by the black and white clock
the hearse arrived
with a cross of flowers
over the coffin.

Sunlight threw patterns
on tall wooden columns.
The memories of Tom
and lost time floooded back
as the hymns were sung
for the young man who forsook
this living and us,
and the funeral address
by an eloquent friend
paid tribute in anecdote
to the Why and Why not
of the boy and the man.

After the blessing
the coffin was turned
and the family followed
the bearers and priest
out to cold sunlight
to the road and the river
which flows through the city
and out to the sea.

OLD MASTER

God took up painting again.
It was more difficult than ever to create a masterpiece
and where should the oldest of masters begin
now that there was also the problem of belatedness,
as well as the new techniques and the critics?
Painting is Dead. God is Dead. They said, they said.
Well, he would prove them wrong himself.
Look, look around at my installations,
the kinetic verve of my constellations,
the videos of my action paintings,
the fluid sculptures in the clouds
and watercolours on every ocean,
but all the self-portraits shook their heads.
They wanted to be the gods instead.

TELEPHONE

For once
God picked up
the telephone.

His number
was ex-directory
given to no one.

He let it ring
three times before
he answered it.

He picked up
the receiver
and remained silent.

The voices
at the other end
sounded familiar,

sounded
like a younger version
of his own godhead.

He hoped
humanity had not
found him.

He listened to
praise abuse questions
hymns prayers sermons screams

birdsong rocksongs
accusations oceans
babble Babel drivel dreams,

all in
a nano-second or so
and then the line went dead.

GUILT

God looked
at the two hands
clasped in prayer.

He saw the fingers,
fingers and thumbs,
of a child-molester

asking forgiveness.
A psychologist,
he read the mind

as it confessed.
Forget it he thought.
You must take what comes.

That night God knelt
and asked forgiveness
of a broken child.

TOAD

Pick him up and he's
a piss-artist out of nappies.
Look at the juice he pees,
terrified of being eaten.

Pulsing panicky dewlap
of double chin,
a stuffed vineleaf,
all mouth and trousers,
he paddles the air
in vain with
inedible thighs
and flipper forepaws.

Amphibious lung
with large malevolent
unblinking eyes,
an obese squat lizard,
discoloured and verrucous,
camouflaged as mud,
slime-green leafmould
or khaki turd.

Jumping genitalia!
Off he goes
to fertilize the ropes
of little toads.

SLOE GIN

The taste reminds me
of being young again.
The stained-glass thimbleful
of purple liquid
is sweet and pungent on the tongue
and the taste is not of plums
but wild blackthorn fruit
picked mature from hedgerows
after the first frosts of autumn.

I am in my grandmother's house.
I have in my hand a glass
of her home-made sloe gin
and we are listening
to Paul Robeson sing
on a wind-up gramophone
as big as a pulpit
while I at eight or nine
am certain what it will be
to feel grown up.

Sloe gin and Old Man River.
The bushes have flowered
and petals fallen
for half a century since then.

GOD IN THE SMALL HOURS

I too wake in the small hours
and think dark thoughts of my own devising.
Remember I do not have your
devious devices and desires
which some of your compatriots
and others confess to me
and I find predictably diverting.
I cannot drink a glass or two of wine
or fantasise about my sexual partners,
past and future, real or imagined,
or worry about money
or whether I shall ever be a grandparent.
Eternity is a long time to contemplate
and does not induce any sense of urgency.
I too remember my mistakes,
catastrophes and aberrations
but I do not have dreams to distract me
or death to defy.

TANGA

Looked like underpants but more so
judging from the pictured torso.
Got my tanga on me now,
rather tight from stern to prow,
tighter than a thong from Tonga,
wish its arms and legs were longer.

Need to be a slimmer swimmer
to tango in this Tesco's tanga,
tangle with the jet-black jockstrap,
strangulating cotton mantrap.
Wish were better hung and younger
when I bought them for a song,
had no inkling when was tinkling
I'd be throttled by a thong.

Looked the word up, eeny-meeny,
'type of very brief bikini',
gives my brief-case other meaning,
breathe in now for paunchy preening.
Half-price bargain tempts a shopper,
now no longer teenybopper
but a grumpy 50 something,
likes home comforts round his whatsit
not a loin-cloth up his coccyx.

Fashion victim inadvertent
not by boxer shorts am curtained
but by tangas left *al fresco*.
Never underpant at Tesco.

Mirror, mirror on the wall
told me pride preceded fall.
Silly me. I'm hardly broke.
Caveat emptor. Pig in poke.
Ponderous buttock, waist-high thigh.
Careful owner, much confused.
Anybody like to buy
six black tangas barely used?

FULL CIRCLE

When forests breathe
and fibres drink
they preconceive
no printer's ink

Inside the rings
of growing bark
we speak our lives
against the dark

Long afterwards
foul papers know
two singing birds
on vanished snow